W9-AGZ-069

Mar '23 8/3/0
Jan '22 5/3/0

Countries We Come From

Greece

by Joyce Markovics

Consultant: Marjorie Faulstich Orellana, PhD
Professor of Urban Schooling
University of California, Los Angeles

BEARPORT
PUBLISHING

New York, New York

Credits

Cover, © Zurijeta/Shutterstock and © Richmatts/iStock; TOC, © Jblah/Dreamstime; 4, © gorillaimages/Shutterstock; 5T, © Poike/iStock; 5B, © Getty Images/iStock; 7, © kostasgr/Shutterstock; 8, © Andrzej Golik/Shutterstock; 9T, © Alxcrs/Shutterstock; 9B, © Pawel Kazmierczak/Shutterstock; 10, © Iakov Filimonov/Shutterstock; 11T, © Lorenzo Patoia/Shutterstock; 11B, © Valentyn Volkov/Shutterstock; 12T, © Lefteris Papaulakis/Shutterstock; 12B, © Sergey Lyashenko/Shutterstock; 13, © Kostas Koutsaftikis/Shutterstock; 14–15, © Emi Cristea/Shutterstock; 15R, © Archives Charmet/Bridgeman Images; 16L, © milangonda/iStock; 16–17, © Anastasios71/Shutterstock; 18, © Lambros Kazan/Shutterstock; 19, © Littleaom/Shutterstock; 20, © Nice_Media/Shutterstock; 21, © Martinan/iStock; 22, © AS Food studio/Shutterstock; 23, © AndrewGorbi/Shutterstock; 24L, © oonair/Shutterstock; 24–25, © caracterdesign/iStock; 26, © George Tsartsianidis/Dreamstime; 27, © IML Image Group Ltd/Alamy Stock Photo; 28, © leungchopan/Shutterstock; 29, © Georgios Alexandris/Shutterstock; 30T, © Tony Kunz/Shutterstock and © spinetta/Shutterstock; 30B, © Shaiith/Shutterstock; 31 (T to B), © Richmatts/iStock, © Anastasios71/Shutterstock, © Ralf Hirsch/Shutterstock, © Andrzej Golik/Shutterstock, © Prof foto 101/Shutterstock, and © Richmatts/iStock; 32, © Lefteris Papaulakis/Shutterstock.

Publisher: Kenn Goin
Senior Editor: Joyce Tavolacci
Creative Director: Spencer Brinker
Design: Debrah Kaiser
Photo Researcher: Thomas Persano

Library of Congress Cataloging-in-Publication Data

Names: Markovics, Joyce L., author.
Title: Greece / by Joyce Markovics.
Description: New York, New York : Bearport Publishing, [2018] | Series:
   Countries we come from | Includes bibliographical references and index. |
   Audience: Ages 5–8.
Identifiers: LCCN 2017014715 (print) | LCCN 2017015089 (ebook) |
ISBN 9781684023103 (ebook) | ISBN 9781684022564 (library)
Subjects: LCSH: Greece—Juvenile literature.
Classification: LCC DF717 (ebook) | LCC DF717 .M265 2018 (print) |
DDC 949.5—dc23
LC record available at https://lccn.loc.gov/2017014715

For more information, write to Bearport Publishing Company, Inc., 45 West 21st Street, Suite 3B, New York, New York 10010. Printed in the United States of America.

10 9 8 7 6 5 4 3 2 1

Contents

This Is Greece 4

Fast Facts. 30

Glossary 31

Index 32

Read More 32

Learn More Online 32

About the Author 32

Spectacular

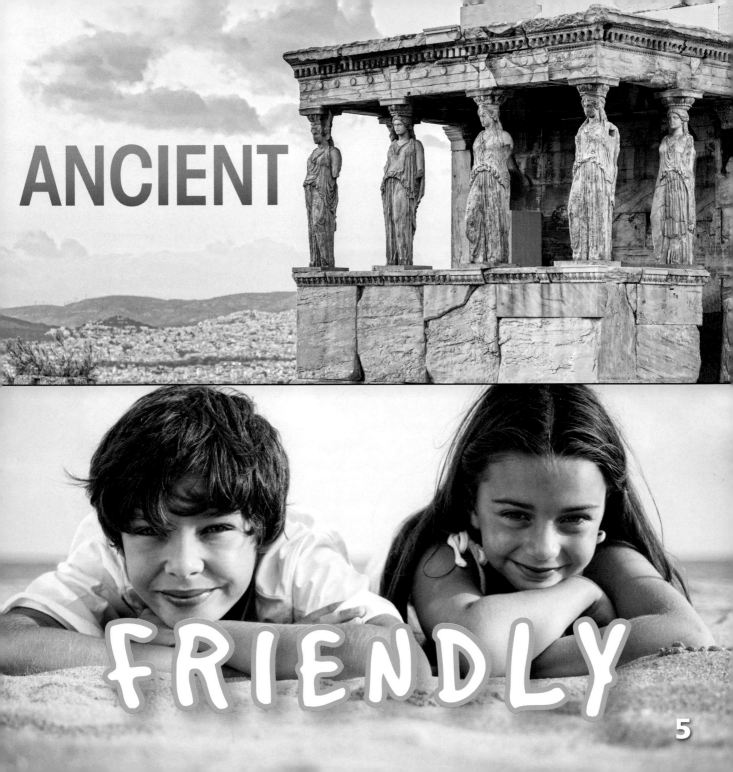

ANCIENT

FRIENDLY

Greece is a country in Europe.

It's surrounded by water.

In addition to the mainland, Greece includes thousands of islands.

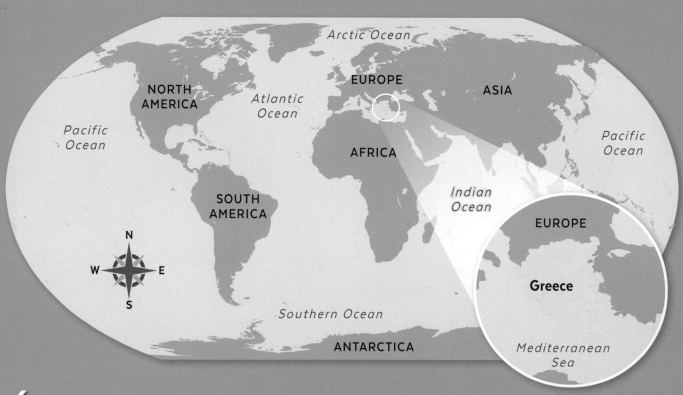

Nearly 11 million people live in Greece.

Greece has deep valleys and tall mountains.

The Vikos **Gorge** dips 3,000 feet (914 m).

Mount Olympus rises more than 9,000 feet (2,743 m)!

Greece is also known for its beautiful beaches.

Much of Greece's land is used for farming.

One of the country's main crops is olives.

Most villages have their own olive **groves**!

olive oil

Ripe olives are pressed to make tasty, golden oil.

Thousands of years ago, people settled in Greece.

Over time, they built a large **civilization**.

a 3,000-year-old Greek artwork

The **ancient** Greeks created the world's first democracy (dih-MOK-*ruh*-see).

In a democracy, people have a say in how they're ruled.

The ancient Greeks built huge cities. They designed tall **temples** with stone columns.

an ancient Greek theater

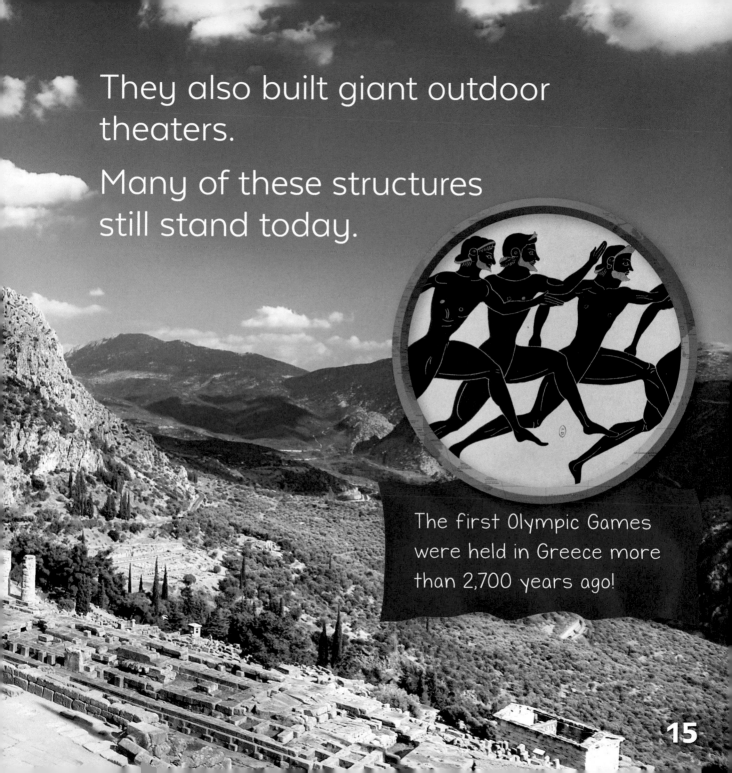

They also built giant outdoor theaters.

Many of these structures still stand today.

The first Olympic Games were held in Greece more than 2,700 years ago!

The **capital** of Greece is Athens.

It's one of the world's oldest cities.

New buildings stand side by side with ancient ones.

Two-thirds of Greeks live in cities.

High above Athens is the Acropolis.

Acropolis means "city at the top" in Greek.

It's a group of very old buildings.

The most famous building is a 2,500-year-old temple called the Parthenon.

The Parthenon is one of the most visited places in Greece.

The main language in Greece is Greek.

This is how you say *hello* and *goodbye*:

Yassou (yah-SOO)

This is how you say *mother*:
Mitera (MEE-teh-ra)

Greek is one of the oldest spoken languages in Europe.

Greek food is delicious! People enjoy flaky spinach pie.

They grill chunks of meat to make souvlaki (soov-LOK-ee).

It's served with creamy yogurt sauce.

The creamy sauce is called tzatziki (tsat-ZEE-kee).

Souvlaki is often wrapped in bread called pita.

Family is the center of Greek life.

Adult children often live with their parents.

Grandparents share the home, too!

Greek families eat most meals together.

Many holidays are celebrated in Greece.

Easter is an important holiday for Christian people.

Families bake special Easter bread.

Greek Easter bread has a dyed red egg baked into it.

People light candles and march through the streets.

Other religions practiced in Greece are Islam and Judaism.

27

Bird-watching is a popular Greek pastime.

More than 440 kinds of birds can be seen in Greece.

Just look up.

Songbirds, swans, and owls all make their homes in Greece.

This bird is called a hoopoe.

Who knows what you might see flying in the sky!

Fast Facts

Capital city: Athens

Population of Greece: Nearly 11 million

Main language: Greek

Money: Euro

Major religion: Christian Orthodox

Neighboring countries include: Albania, Bulgaria, Macedonia, and Turkey

Cool Fact: The ancient Greeks thought it was bad luck to eat beans!

ancient (AYN-shunt) very old

capital (KAP-uh-tuhl) a city where a country's government is based

civilization (siv-uh-luh-ZEY-shuhn) an advanced society of people

gorge (GORJ) a deep, narrow space between rocky cliffs

groves (GROHVZ) groups of fruit trees

temples (TEM-puhlz) buildings used for worship

Index

buildings 14–15,
    16–17, 18–19
capital 16–17, 30
cities 14, 16–17,
    18, 30
family 24–25

farming 10–11
food 10–11,
    22–23, 24,
    26, 30
history 12–13,
    14–15, 18–19

holidays 26–27
land 6, 8–9, 10
language 20–21,
    30
Olympic Games 15
population 7, 30

Read More

Robinson, Joanna J. *Greece
(One World, Many Countries).*
New York: Child's World (2016).

Spilsbury, Richard. *Discover
Greece (Discover Countries).* North
Mankato, MN: Capstone (2012).

Learn More Online

To learn more about Greece, visit
www.bearportpublishing.com/CountriesWeComeFrom

About the Author

Joyce Markovics lives along the Hudson River.
She once traveled to the Greek island of Samos
to visit a great computer scientist and friend, Stamatis
Vassiliadis (1951–2007). He is deeply missed by all.